HOW TO ANALYZE PEOPLE

The simple guide to quickly read people's.

Oliver Bennet

Table of Contents – How to analyze people

Introduction

How do I analyze people? Do I need to follow any formula to do this? Is there a particular approach that is helpful to understand people? When it comes to understanding a human being's personality traits, there are many different theories and models, which can be followed. You can understand one's personality based on his or her body language, inborn personality traits, facial features, etc. Some say you can even get to know about a person by the way he or she walks.

All the above-cited theories are 100 percent true. But there are so many other factors to be considered when it comes to analyzing people and their underlying behavioral traits. You will need to have a deeper knowledge on many other things before concluding on a person's personality and character.

Let us try to understand on how to analyze one's personality using a practical illustration.

Practical Illustration on Analyzing People

There was this guy in the gym that was always punctual. He used to come to the gym every day at the same time. Well, what is so great about that, you ask? If you are not looking at the smallest of the details, you will end up losing the basic and important personality traits of a person. Coming back to our gym guy, the detail cited might seem unimportant. But for someone who knows how to analyze people, this simple detail can mean a lot.

This guy's punctuality shows the following personality traits in him:

- Self-motivated

- Strong willed

- Well organized

- Knows the importance of time

All the above-said traits are visible because of how he handles time to be punctual not just once but regularly. He is not a procrastinator but a doer.

The next important thing that was noticeable in this guy was he always wore clothes that showcased his muscles. The exercises and the workout process he followed were also quite strange. It was not the common one's people usually do, but there was an odd style to his routine. This meant that the guy was quite a show-off and wanted to be the center of attraction. Further information confirmed that he was the only child in the family.

When you try to analyze one's personality, it is important to note how their birth order affects the personality. When a person is the only child in the family, they are usually showered with loads of love and attention during their childhood. Sometimes, this continues even after they grow up. Since they are used to being the center of attraction in their family, they expect the same wherever they go.

Another important thing about this gym guy was that he always wore black. I guess he loved to wear black! Though he often kept changing his clothes during his workout routine, all his clothes were black or had black shades in them. Even the cover of his mobile was black.

While analyzing one's personality, it is important to understand that people will go to an extreme if they try to escape from something. It was the same with the gym guy too. Wearing black revealed that the guy wanted to appear dangerous, tough and evil. He wanted to look like a bad boy.

Further information on the guy confirmed the reason for this – the other kids bullied him when he was a little boy. He felt weak. While growing up, he ensured he concealed his past by playing tough. Working out regularly at the gym and donning black were the two steps he had taken to help him run away from his childhood.

It is important to connect all the dots when you are analyzing someone's personality. You need to keep in mind that these dots are the ones, which will lead you to the finishing line.

If our assumptions are true, our gym guy wanted to be powerful and tried all the other means that would help him become powerful. So, he should be doing other things apart from going to the gym. The guess was right – our gym guy was interested in martial arts and was practicing this regularly.

When a person wants to move towards an imperative goal, he gets interested in things that help him in the process. In other words, he or she would want to get away from the identity he hates, i.e., being weak, being scared, being anxious, etc.

Is It Easy to Analyze People?

It would be foolish if it were told that reading couple of articles on analyzing people would help you understand anyone and everyone's personality and behavior traits. The good news is that all the knowledge required for you to analyze people can be found in books and articles. All you have to do is understand the basics and implement them in the right way.

The first and foremost thing you need to do is – read all possible articles on human psychology, personality analysis and behavioral traits. You will then need to test your knowledge by analyzing your personality. When you are successful at doing this, you can try the approach with your best friend or spouse or siblings. Try to analyze him or her.

When you are confident and know the outcome is correct, you can start implementing what you learned from other people – especially strangers.

Another Example to Understand the Concept Better

There was this girl in our project who was always seen accompanying guys rather than other girls. She was, in fact, more comfortable talking with the opposite gender and loved discussing guy-related topics. She enjoyed the conversation and always came out with accurate details on whatever topic she discoursed. A normal girl would have found those topics boring, but for her it was different.

While analyzing her behavior, it was confirmed that she didn't like her feminine role because of which she was trying to mask herself with another role. What would be the reason for doing this? Collecting further information on her background gave us the answer we needed.

She grew up in a house where women were valued less than men. Since her childhood, she saw the men in the family being treated differently compared to women. This was the core reason for her to protest against her gender.

The most crucial thing you need to understand while analyzing people's behavior is – to study their childhood, the way they were brought up, their experiences as a kid, etc. The experiences one has during their young age can permanently affect their future behavior.

Coming back to our girl, she often kept saying that she was particularly interested in zodiac signs, as most of her traits resembled what her zodiac sign said. We often try to compensate the things we lack by focusing on things we always wanted. In this case, the girl lacked self-understanding because she had developed this extreme interest in zodiac signs. She wanted to compensate for the lack of knowledge she had about self.

The important factor you need to note when you are analyzing people's behavior is that humans tend to turn their attention toward something that helps them compensate for their weaknesses.

More analysis on the girl's behavior:

This girl always used to challenge people and was extremely competitive at work. She ensured that anything she started was always completed on time and to a good standard. Being the youngest kid in the family, she was always surrounded by siblings who had already proved their mettle in a specific area. She had to stand out from those capable grown-ups. This led to the extremely competitive behavior, which was necessary to compensate for her weakness.

While analyzing people's behavior, it is necessary to relate to their birth order. This will help you understand the basic traits of the person. Another peculiar thing in this girl's case was, even though she was a strong-willed, extroverted and competitive woman, she got married to a guy who was a complete opposite to her character. Her husband was reserved and shy. He was not very confident when compared to the girl.

This proves that our analysis has been true so far. Since her childhood, she was taught that women were weak and not as important as men. This made her hate being a woman. As she grew up into an adult, she specifically became attracted to weak men as that would give her the chance to be the dominant member in the family.

The last and final thing one should note while analyzing people's behavior is that most humans are not aware of their personality dynamics. In the case of this girl, she could never understand why she was attracted to weak men. The reason is all these personality dynamics happen at a subconscious level.

Personality and Behavior

You don't need to spend months or years with a person to know their personality. All you have to do is understand the simple principles about a person's behavior. This will help you to start noticing their underlying personality, which gets revealed in many circumstances. It can be tiny actions, which are usually not given importance by others. There will not be any change in these behaviors even though the time passes.

For example, if your best friend loves bungee jumping, it means this person will never hesitate to take any kind of risk. It doesn't necessarily need to be only physical risk. He can even quit his job because he simply didn't like the job. He won't wait to find another job even though his financial security is at risk.

On the contrary, if a person sits at the same place in the same food court every day, he might fear change. He will get restless or anxious when it comes to a new routine or new environment. He will maximize efforts to resist the change when it is about to happen and find an escape mechanism. For instance, if he is moved to a new team or a new work profile or gets a new boss, he will most likely resist the change.

Let's say a person keeps looking toward both the sides of the road many times before she decides to cross the road. Then the lady would most probably be very cautious. She would be careful and reserved when it comes to decision-making. And even if she takes a risk, it will be a well-calculated risk.

If a person likes to stick to a particular job without wanting to change it, it is possible that he or she would be loyal and stick to his or her partner until the end.

These tiny and minute details, which seem to be of no value, provide good clarity of a person's behavior in serious and difficult situations.

Chapter 1:   Behavioral Psychology

From a psychological viewpoint, human behavior concerns the full spectrum of emotional and physical behaviors that humans engage in that include social, biological, and intellectual actions and are impacted by attitudes, culture, ethics, rapport, and genetics, among other considerations. Human behavior is a complex interplay of cognition, actions, and emotion. Correspondingly, actions are behavior as actions capture everything that can be observed. Actions can be captured through eyes or physiological sensors. An initiation or transition from one state to another is an action. Actions as behaviors can happen at various time scales starting from sweat gland activity to muscular activation, sleep, or food consumption.

For cognition as behavior, cognition defines thoughts and mental images that one carries and can be both nonverbal and verbal. For instance, "I have to work on my book" can be treated as verbal cognition. On the other hand, imagine how your project will look after reworking on it is considered as a nonverbal cognition. As such, cognitions consist of skills and knowledge by knowing how to apply tools in a constructive manner, such as memorizing a jacket's color or singing songs.

When viewing emotions as behavior, emotions are considered a relatively brief conscious experience marked by intense mental activity and a feeling that is not influenced by either knowledge or reasoning. Emotions normally happen from a positive to negative scale. Increased arousal can cause other aspects of physiology that indicate emotional processing, such as enhanced respiration rate. Emotions can only be inferred indirectly akin to cognition through monitoring facial expressions and tracking arousal, among others.

Understanding Behavior from a Psychological Viewpoint

Investment Model

Human behavior can be understood in terms of work effort focused on creating change. For instance, whether Hilda is headed out due to the need to watch the movie or wants to be with her boyfriend, the act of going to the movie is a form of investment. In this manner, human behavior occurs due to the need to get a particular outcome. The return of this investment can be found from the movie Hilda watches or a kiss from her boyfriend at the end of it.

In this aspect, behavior involves considering the investment in terms of calories, time, risks, and opportunity costs. The motivation of where to invest our actions in spurring a particular behavior to emanate from evolutionary influences that have made us prioritize sex, food, safety, territory, and higher social status over other states of affairs. Genetics also impact certain behavioral traits, such as dispositions and temperaments. For instance, extroverted people find stimulating social situations more satisfying compared to introverted people. Against this backdrop, the learning history of an individual impact the investment value system. For instance, if Hilda loved the first two Star Wars movies, we can expect her to show a strong desire to see the third.

An illustration of human behavior's investment model is where one is seated on a sofa gazing at the television when an advert of a cookie triggers in you the desire to pour a cup of milk. You have had a tough day, and you are feeling burnt out. In your mind, a small computation takes place where you weigh on the value of getting up and pouring yourself a glass of milk. Eventually, the thirst wins out, and you decide to get a glass of milk from the refrigerator. Unfortunately, a quick look in the fridge indicates there is no milk, which makes you take a glance at the rubbish you have, and you see that you've already used all the milk bottles.

The feeling that follows this disruption in your ability to fulfill your desire is irritation, and your first thought then is to overcome this obstacle by running to the store and getting a bottle. You then juxtapose this idea with the cost in terms of time, effort, and money that would cost you, and you drop the idea. Still, you must satiate your desire for a drink somehow, so you decide to drink some orange juice instead. In detail, the investment model for understanding human behavior views behaviors in the form of energy and labor required to realizing a particular outcome — the behavior costs in the form of time and energy computed in the form of benefits and costs. Human behavior is largely a cost-benefit analysis according to the investment model of animal behavior. Most animal documentaries on animals' behavior can help you realize how inherently animals make the cost-benefit analysis.

Take the case of wildebeests in African savanna plains that need to drink water and cross the infested river with hungry crocodiles. In this environment, water and grass are scarce, and wildebeests desperately need water and grass. Simultaneously, the wildebeests have to watch out for marauding crocodiles lurking under the surface of the water, ready to devour the wildebeests. Eventually, wildebeests have to invoke an investment model of behavior to maximize the possibility of living, drinking water, and crossing the river to graze. Under this model, most wildebeests cautiously approach the river, ensuring that they near the river bank when drinking water, which would enable them to retract sporadically at the hint of any threat that might put them out of control and in danger.

In this manner, human behavior is a sort of transaction with the environment. The human being actions are primed to maximize benefits from the environment. The mind is a critical component of behavior as it stores a history of what has desired outcomes and computing the cost-benefit analysis before one-acts. It can be argued that the investment model of behavior affirms the assumption that human behavior is conscious and well thought. Additionally, actions lead to lost opportunities, and one has to pursue an action that best maximizes the intended outcomes. For instance, if an animal spends time defending a territory, it loses out on finding food.

Social Influence Model of Human Behavior

Human behavior can be viewed from the understanding that a human being is a social animal. Human behavior happens in the context of a social matrix. A social influence entails the actions that influence the investment of another person. For instance, when Hilda was going to the movie, she asked her boyfriend out, or the boyfriend did ask her out.

In most cases, social influence processes involve cooperation, cooperation, and whether the transactions move people closer or make them drift apart. Social influence also manifests as a resource. As a resource, social influence concerns the capacity to move other people in alignment with our interests. Social influence in this context refers to the levels of social and respect value other people show us and the degree to which they listen, care about our well-being, and sacrifice for us. For instance, if Hilda is attracted to his boyfriend and agrees to go to the movie with her, this indicates social influence. If the boyfriend breaks up with Hilda, it is a potent indication of a social influence loss.

Additionally, social influence is determined by the amount of attention from other people. In line with this understanding, a person's actions will seek to attract attention from people or sustain the attention of people. Probably you have colleagues or public figures that consistently act to attract and sustain admiration from other people. On a personal level, one is likely to act in a manner that invites admiration from colleagues, friends, and other people. The behavior and likely behavior of an individual is likely to optimize admiration from others. Furthermore, within the social influence model of human behavior, people are likely to act in a manner that invites more positive emotions than others' negative emotions. In a way, the need to attract more positive emotions from others is related to attracting admiration from others, but it is highly related to emotional intelligence. One can only enhance the likelihood of getting a positive emotional reaction from others if they have requisite emotional intelligence levels.

Through emotional intelligence, one learns to show empathy and pay attention to how others are feeling. Against this backdrop, human behavior is likely to be reactive to how others are feeling. It is likely to be highly considerate of others for the motivation to attract positive emotions from them. This can also become highly performative, as human behavior also makes people sacrifice their needs for other people to gain more influence through it. People who can gather a lot of social influence are generally able to have power over others to have hundreds of people who will willingly sacrifice their own needs for them. This means that this person in power is also aware that there are so many people who would do anything to associate with their influence, and their behavior stems from this knowledge. On the other hand, the influential people's followers are likely to take the actions of the individual as guidance or a message of how one should act and live.

Justification Model of Human Behavior

First, human behavior requires justifications by legitimizing it. For instance, when you shout at someone, there are chances that one will qualify the behavior by stating that they were upset. In reaching a justification, one assesses the behavior and the ideal outcome. For instance, the ideal outcome may have attracted admiration from others, but one ended up embarrassing themselves in public. Expectedly, the individual will feel angry for not only failing to attain an ideal reaction from the audience but also degrading the status quo. In this state, the individual will justify subsequent undesired behavior by drawing attention to the disappointment they got earlier on.

Using the Hilda and the movie example, Hilda may have felt justified to make her boyfriend tag along to the movie and allow the boyfriend to show romance because of what lovers do. The justification of her behavior and the boyfriend's behavior emanates from observation and learned patterns of what lovers do and not necessarily how they feel. Justification of behavior can be simply that others do, so the individual is obliged to emulate the same. Try watching court proceedings for you to realize how people place significant value of justification for their behavior.

At the corporate level, organizations have invested significantly in assessing human behavior during recruitment stages and assessing workers. Human behavior is complex, and organizations seek to have the best bet to recruit and retain fairly predictable workers. Most of the personality tests administered during hiring and appraisal processes are meant to help profile workers and have a predictable look at how they may behave. There have been attempts to determine a formula for human behavior as a simple system, but it has been satisfactorily concluded that human behavior is dynamic.

Chapter 2:   How You Can Analyze the Behavior of People

Studying people is not reserved for psychiatrists but any other person even though psychiatrists are best positioned to analyze people. Analyzing people requires understanding verbal and nonverbal cues. When studying people, you should try to remain objective and be open to new information. Nearly each one of us has some form of personal biases and stereotypes that blocks our ability to understand another person correctly. When analyzing an individual, it is crucial to reconcile that information against the profession and cultural demands on the target person. Some environments may force an individual to exhibit particular behavior that is not necessarily part of their real one.

Start by analyzing the body language cues of the target person you are trying to read. Body language provides the most authoritative emotional and physiological status of an individual. It is difficult to rehearse all forms of body language, which makes body language critical in understanding a person. Verbal communication can be faked through rehearsal and experience, and this can give misleading stand. When examining body language, analyze the different types of body language as a set. For instance, analyze facial expressions, body posture, pitch, tonal variation, touch and eye contact, as a related but different manifestation of communication and emotional status. For instance, when tired, one is likely to stretch their arms and rest on the left and right tops of adjacent chairs, sit in a slumped position, stare at the ceiling, and drop their heads. Analyzing only one aspect of body language can mislead one to come up with a conclusion correctly.

Additionally, it would be best if you give attention to appearance. The first impression counts, but it can also be misleading. In formal contexts, an individual's appearance is critical to communicate the professionalism of the person and the organizational state of mind of that individual. For example, an individual with an unbuttoned shirt indicates he hurried or is casual with the audience and the message. Wearing formal attire buttoned and tucked in suggests prior preparation and seriousness that the person lends to the occasion. Having unkempt hair may indicate a rebellious mind, and this might be common among African professors in Africa, for instance. In most settings, having unkempt hair suggests that one lacks the discipline to prepare for the formal context or is overworked and busy. Lack of expected grooming may indicate an individual battling with life challenges or feeling uncared for.

It is also important that one should take note of the posture of the person. Posture communicates a lot about the involvement of an individual in a conversation. Having an upright posture suggests eagerness and active participation in what is being communicated. If one cups their face in the arms and lets the face rest on both thighs, it suggests that one feels exhausted or has deviated from the conversation completely. Having crossed arms suggests defensiveness or deep thought. One sitting in a slumped position suggests that he/she is tired and not participating in the ongoing conversation. Leaning on the wall or any object suggests casualness that the person is lending to an ongoing conversation.

If at home, sitting with crossed legs suggests that one is completely relaxed. However, the same posture at the workplace suggests that one is feeling tensed and at the same time concentrating.

Furthermore, observe the physical movements in terms of distance and gestures. The distance between you and the target individual communicates about the level of respect and assurance that the individual perceives. A social distance is the safest bet when communicating, and it suggests high levels of professionalism or respect between the participants. Human beings tend to be territorial as exhibited by the manner that they guard their distance. Any invasion of the personal distance will make the individual defensive and unease with the interaction.

For this reason, when an individual shows discomfort when the distance between communicators is regarded as social or public, then the individual may have other issues bothering him or her. Social and public distances should make one feel fully comfortable. Allowing a person close enough or into the personal distance suggests that the individual feels secure and familiar with the other person. Through reading, the distance between the communicators will give a hint on the respect, security, and familiarity between the individuals and the likely profession of the individuals.

Correspondingly, then try to read facial expressions as deep frown lines indicate worry or over-thinking. Facial expressions are among the visible and critical forms of body language and tell more about an individual's true emotional status. For instance, twitching the mouth suggests that an individual is not listening

17

and is showing disdain to the speaker. A frozen face indicates that the person is shell-shocked, which can happen when making a presentation of health and diseases or when releasing results of an examination. A smiling face with the smile not being prolonged communicates that one is happy and following the conversation. A prolonged smile suggests sarcasm. If one continually licks, the lips may indicate that one is lying or feeling disconnected from the conversation.

Relatedly, try to create a baseline for what merits as normal behavior. As you will discover, people have distinct mannerisms that may be misleading to analyze them as part of the communication process. For instance, some individuals will start a conversation by looking down or at the wall before turning to the audience. Mildly, mannerisms are like a ritual that one must activate before they make a delivery. Additionally, each person uniquely expresses the possible spectra of body language. By establishing a baseline of normal behavior, one gets to identify and analyze deviations from the standardized normal behavior accurately. Against this understanding, one will not erratically score a speaker that shuffles first if that is part of his behavior when speaking to an audience.

Furthermore, pay attention to inconsistencies between the established baseline that you have created and the individual's gestures and words. Once you have created a baseline, then examine for any deviations from this baseline. For instance, if one speaks in a high-pitched voice that is uncharacteristically of the individual, the person may feel irritated. If one normally walks across the stage when speaking but the individual chooses to speak from a fixed position during the current speech, the person is exhibiting a deviation that may suggest that the individual is having self-awareness or is feeling unease with the current audience. If an individual speaks fast, but usually the person speaks with a natural flow, the person is in a hurry or has not prepared for it.

Correspondingly, view gestures as clusters to elicit a meaning of what the person is communicating or trying to hide. When speaking a person, will express different gestures and dwelling on the current gesture may make you arrive at a misleading conclusion. Instead, one should view the gestures as clusters and interpret what they imply. For instance, if a speaker throws the hands randomly in the air, raises one of their feet, stamps the floor, and shakes his or her hands, all of these could suggest a speaker feeling irked and disappointed by the audience or the message. As such, different aspects of body language should be interpreted as a unit rather than in isolation.

Go further and try to recognize the strong voice. A strong voice suggests the authority and confidence of the speaker. If the speaker lacks a strong voice, he or she is new to what is being presented or has stage fright. Having a strong voice that is not natural suggests a spirited attempt to appear in charge and confident. A strong voice should be natural if the individual feels composed and confident in what he or she is talking about.

Relatedly, observe how the individual walks. When speaking to a target person, they will walk across the stage or make movements around the site where the conversation is happening. From the manner of walking, we can read a lot about the individual.

Walking up and down while speaking to an audience may indicate panic or spirited attempts to appear in control. Speaking while walking slowly across the stage from one end to the other end indicates that one is comfortable speaking to the audience. If a member of the audience poses a question and walks towards the individual, it suggests interest in clarifying what the individual is asking.

It might be necessary to scout for personality cues. Fortunately, all people have identifiable personalities, but these can be difficult to read for a person not trained in a psychologist. However, through observation, one will get cues on the personality of the individual. For instance, an outgoing person is likely to show a warm smile and laugh at jokes. A socially warm person is likely to want to make personal connections when speaking, such as mentioning a particular person in the audience. Reserved individuals are likely to use fewer words in their communication and appear scared or frozen on stage when speaking.

Additionally, one should listen to intuition, as it is often valid. Gut feelings are often correct, and when reading a person, you should give credence to your gut feeling about the person. When reading a person and you get a feeling that the person is socially warm, you should entertain this profiling while analyzing the person's body language. While considering gut feeling, you should classify it under subjective analysis, as it is not based on observable traits and behaviors but an inner feeling.

Expectedly, watch the eye contact. Creating eye contact suggests eagerness and confidence in engaging the audience. Avoiding eye contact suggests stage fright and shyness and lack confidence in what one is talking about. A sustained look is a stare, intended to intimidate, or may suggest absentmindedness of the individual. If one continuously blinks eyes while looking at a target person suggests a flirting behavior. An eye contact that gradually drops to the individual's chest and thigh suggests a deviation of thoughts from the conversation.

Additionally, pay attention to touch. The way a person shakes hands speaks a lot about their confidence and formality. A firm handshake that is brief indicates confidence and professionalism. A weak handshake that is brief indicates that one is feeling unease. On the other hand, a prolonged handshake, whether weak or strong, suggests that the person is trying to flirt with you, especially between opposite sexes. Touching someone on the head may suggest rudeness and should be avoided.

Lastly, listen to the tone of voice and laughter. Laughing may mean happiness or sarcasm. Americans are good at expressing sarcastic laughter, and it is achieved by changing the tones of the laughter. The tone of the voice states if the person is feeling authoritative and confident or not. Overall, a tonal variation infers that the individual is speaking naturally and convincingly. A flat tone specifies a lack of self-confidence and unfamiliarity with the conversation or audience and should be avoided.

Chapter 3:   Deconstructing Behaviors

Human behavior is the reaction of a human being to internal or external stimuli; this means that your behavior is how you react to your environment, whether internal or external. It is made up of all the physical activities and emotions that you express as you respond to these environmental stimulations. The human behavior is transient, and changes as the person grows until it becomes more rigid. Behavior is how we can look into your mind, figure out what you are thinking, and think those thoughts. It helps us see your attitude towards certain circumstances and respond individually and then collectively as a human. Humans all share similar behavior and have individual expressions. Behavior also can help us into your culture, social interactions, values or paradigms, ethics, persuasions, views that you hold dear to you, which is the authorities that influence your thought patterns.

Now that we have defined what behavior is, we also need to understand certain behavioral measurements that we have. If an organism expresses itself, we want to be sure the organism is expressing itself in the confines of acceptable and customary behaviors. We have common behaviors, unusual, acceptable, and some that we cannot tolerate at all. How do we know certain behaviors are acceptable? These things are defined for us by our societies. The society forms the framework by which our habits are screened through the popular thought "do we do this here?", "Is this what people of our society do?" "Is this out of place here?" these form some of the basic thoughts that go into the acceptance or rejection of certain social behaviors. For instance, cannibalism is acceptable in fewer cultures today, even cultures that practiced it before, have abolished the practice. It means eating meat raw could be seen as awkward and out of place. Psychology, sociology, anthropology, and economics are centered behavioral fields. They deal with human behavior concerning social interactions.

Because our environment highly influences behavior, it is possible for it to change, if those environmental factors that trigger them are absent. For instance, if staying in a hot environment would always force one to detest wearing clothes. If this individual moved to a colder region, the individual would have to adopt a new way to survive due to environmental factors. Behavior changes as the individual moves through life and encounters myriad environments and niches that incite certain reactions. Even though behavior could change, there are some intrinsic parts of the human that cannot change. After all, the behavior is a reaction of the person to his environment. If that's the case, then behavior can also be influenced by genetic and physiological traits. These traits have moved psychologists to classify behavior into different catalogs with their different reactions.

Let's quickly look at the factors that influence our behavior

The manner at which a person handles a situation personally, or maybe in a gathering, is influenced by many factors, but we would look at those key ones; those that have a primary role to play in how a person relates with another reacts to a situation.

Abilities

Abilities cut across talents and skills, and whatever you can do that fascinates. Skills are things that a person learns from his environment, while talents are intrinsic and innate. Examples of talents are singing, dancing, drawing, etc. talents are normally things you are not taught to do, they are things that just flow naturally or don't need so much natural input to spark up. This means that if it is a talent, while learning, it would be easier to absorb than when it is not. A skill, on the other hand, is gotten through hard work and consistency. For instance, you have driving as a skill, or writing, etc. these things are not innate. They are learned. You can transform your talent into a skill, in what way? By refining it till it becomes marketable. They don't just stop at being skills and talents, and they are more abilities that we humans possess, abilities like intellectual and physical abilities. Your intellectual abilities tend to influence your behavior so much; how you process information and how you conclude would affect how you behave. Let me add something about learning here; if you have a scenario with an educated person and a non-educated person, they will react differently. You would rarely have an educated person eat of the trash because he/she knows the dangers. Verbal, reasoning, memory—cognitive abilities greatly influence one's behavior.

Gender and Genetics

A human's genes are the basic building blocks for existence. What this means is, locked up in your genes is information on how your body would form. From the moment the spermatozoa of your father were released, it carried in its genetic information that would impact how you would look and how you would behave. In them were codes that contained the entire wiring of your human being. Genetics are the reason for gender. Gender, in general, is whether a human is male or female as defined by society. What this means is that societal accepted parameters define our genders. For instance, a human with a penis is called male because of the presence (majorly) of the penis, and a human with a vagina and breasts is called a woman, because of the presence of her sexual organ. Our gender affects our behavior. Men have the way they act, and women have the way they act. The truth is, because of the presence of certain hormones in excess in our system, like the presence of estrogen makes women act in a certain way, and testosterone makes men behave in a certain way.

Race & Culture

Culture is the eyes through which we see the world. Our culture greatly influences how we react to the world. Our culture is our way of life, not just us, but the way of life of the people who live with and around us. It is the way of life that we have come to see and accept as safe and important. Although some cultural practices have been rendered obsolete due to enlightenment, another culture can be born and practiced. For instance, if a person belongs to a culture where they do not allow women to take up leadership roles, they would react to women as secondary. If he belongs to another culture where the women are allowed to lead, and his supreme leader is a woman, he would not be taught to subjugate women. This is the impact of culture. It forms our worldview. We see the world from our cultural lens; if a person is African, he relates to the world that way. This is what makes nature beautiful, the fact that we all have different cultures, and if a person looks at the world from these different perspectives, the world takes on a new shape. It can broaden your mind and your perspective. Looking through various cultures can help you value humanity and what humanity has to offer. It gives a less selfish perspective.

Perception

Perception is the method the mind engages in changing stimuli into meaningful information bits that it can use. This means that if you see something, or hear something, perception is how you take that thing you heard and transform it into something very useful to you. For instance, if you hear your name that is an external stimulus or sound from your environment, your brain would take that stimulus and translate it into something you can understand—your name—and you would respond.

Perception can be dividing into six parts, namely:

Sound perception: this is the ability to perceive/interpret different sounds and sound waves in the environment and is aided by the ears and the brain.

Perception of speech: this is the ability to interpret sound to hear into meaningful bits of information that can be used in communication.

The perception of touch is how humans use their bodies to identify objects and relate to their physical environment through touch.

Perception of taste: Humans can identify different flavors by tasting with their tongue and smelling with their nose. There is an apparatus called taste buds that are used for sensing and identifying tastes in the tongue.

Perception of smell: this is the ability of a human to identify different scents of objects or odors in the environment through their nose. This helps the human receive stimuli from the environment and translate it into a smell. Why do we need to smell? Imagine you were in a room full of chemicals that could harm you, but you could not identify them as harmful from their smell?

Perception of sight: this is the ability of humans to sense objects as they move through light. It is the eye's reaction to light to reveal our environment to us. This ability helps us navigate our environment to avoid obstacles and identify threats.

Religion and Spirituality

Religion is one of the world's greatest influences. It has influenced men so much, and many can kill or die for what they believe. This deep-seated awareness that a creator exists and a need to worship him has changed our behaviors all through the ages. Religion is a deep part of our culture; in fact, most cultures are built around religious beliefs. For instance, the Christian faith frowns at murder, marrying more than one wife, engaging in intercourse before marriage or outside of marriage.

Types of Behavior: there are two broad types of human behaviors. That is, there are just two ways human beings interact with the world in a broad sense. The first is the extrovert, and the other is the introvert. There are other ways to analyze human behavior that other psychologists have identified. Some identify four behavioral types, other identify six. Still, the underlying factor is that amongst all the behavioral expression, they are either very expressive (extroverts) or they aren't as expressive, they are more of the enclosed personality type (introverts). The basic tools in analyzing any behavior first is to know what these behaviors look like. How does an introvert act like, and how does an extrovert act like? If you can figure these out, it would be easy to analyze them according to their behavior.

For instance, it already an obvious fact that an extrovert is expressive, and an introvert is not. It is also obvious that specific behavioral terms cannot fit some people. Some people act like introverts in some situations, and in some other cases, they are extroverted. You must also know that there are degrees to these things. Some people are extreme introverts, and some that are not. These behavioral patterns have their strengths and weaknesses. As you read along, find those strengths and build on them. If you focus on the weakness, you might hurt your growth and progress.

Chapter 4: How to Use Emotional Intelligence to Analyze Anyone?

What Is Emotional Intelligence?

Emotional intelligence is recognizing emotions and leveraging on personal information in making healthy choices. Emotional intelligence is the capacity to acknowledge our emotions, regulate them, discern others' feelings, and differentiate between varying emotions, and using emotional intelligence, you can facilitate thoughts and behavior to achieve the desired results.

Since emotional intelligence involves recognizing emotions, it is essential to understand what emotions are and what types of emotions there are.

What Are Emotions?

These are mental states or feelings that occur spontaneously and not by intention. Physiological reactions often accompany these feelings. These occurrences respond to our perception of what is happening or what we see or hear per-time. Emotions help us understand our experiences. We would never know that a loved one's death is a painful experience if we have never felt sadness. We would never know that someone destroying our lawn is an annoying experience if we have never felt angry. Feeling emotions help us categorize our experiences and react accordingly. Positive emotions register an experience we are having or are about to have as good and worth having. When we say we look forward to the experience, it is not the experience we look forward to per sé. It is more the emotions associated with that experience that we look forward to having.

On the other hand, negative emotions alert us of unpleasant or potentially unpleasant experiences. We know we should do certain things or not do certain things if we would avoid such experiences. For example, when faced with a sudden threat, we feel fear of loss or pain. The emotion of fear triggers a fight or flight reaction. What we are trying to avoid is the loss or pain, not the occurrence itself.

Without emotions, there would be no emotional intelligence. Without emotional intelligence, we would not tell precisely the kinds of experiences we want to have and the kinds we don't want to have.

According to author David G. Meyers, "Emotion is made up of three components; physiological arousal, conscious experience and expressive behaviors." Physiological arousal means the person feeling a particular emotion will become physiologically alert. This is a point where the sense organs are stimulated to perceive. A brain primarily controls physiological arousal called the reticular activating system (RAS).

Expressive behavior refers to a behavioral reaction to the perception of what is happening or what is seen, heard or thought. This often involves verbal and non-verbal communication of a person's emotions.

Conscious Experience refers to the awareness of a person's environment, what he sees, hears and feels, and his thoughts.

Emotional intelligence is impactful in every part of your life. These are four areas it can affect.

1) Your performance at work

Most people keep their emotions at the door when going to work to appear more professional, although it used to seem that way. Emotions have always been in the workplace, but they were kept in check, with people pretending not to feel while they are working.

2) Your health physically

If you're unable to put in control your stress levels, it can manifest physically, and it can lead to serious health issues. Uncontrolled stress can cause an increase in your blood pressure, it can weaken the immune system, it can increase the risk of heart attack and stroke, it is also one of the leading causes of infertility, and ages on quickly.

The first step to improving your emotional intelligence is to learn how to relieve stress. Learn How to take breaks when you are under pressure.

3) Your relationships

If you understand your emotions and control them, you will be better at expressing how you feel and understanding how others are feeling.

This allows you to communicate more effectively and form stronger relationships, both at work and in your personal life.

How Improving Your Emotional Intelligence Can Be Beneficial To You

Being able to maintain control of your emotions will help you in every area of your life. It helps you manage your emotions and feelings when you are in stressful or emotional situations and avoid unnecessary dramas. You'd be able to make decisions without being influenced by your present emotions. You'd be able to make logical decisions devoid of emotions.

To improve your emotional intelligence and decision-making abilities, you need to understand and learn how to manage your emotions by developing critical skills needed to control and manage overwhelming stress, and communication effectively. If you can control your feelings, you can control your life

Indicators of High Emotional Intelligence

There are different measures of EI depending on which model you are looking at. Some companies have their human resources departments run the tests on applicants and employees as a requisite for hiring or retention. While this is so, there are still criticisms about the accuracy and methodology of the diagnostic tools. However, in practical terms, experts have come up with their lists of what traits or characteristics people who are highly emotionally intelligent have.

Among the more commonly listed qualities include:

Ability to Label His Emotions Correctly – there are many possible variations and combinations of the basic emotions. Being able to accurately label these emotions lead to more rational choices and decisions. Misunderstandings and counterproductive reactions are avoided.

When you gain mastery of your emotions, you can describe your less than cheery mood as more than just "down" or "sad." You will be able to say that you are "dejected," "lonely," or "nostalgic." All these variegations of "sad" have different meanings. When you label your emotions accurately, you can get deeper into the cause of your emotional state.

Awareness of What He Can and Cannot Do– self-awareness is one of the foundations of emotional intelligence. When you have a high EI, you will have a heightened awareness of your strengths and weaknesses.

People with high EI accept that they have limitations and can devise a plan to work around those limitations not to accomplish their goals. They capitalize on their strengths to propel them towards success faster. They are confident enough of their capabilities to laugh off mistakes and joke about themselves.

Natural Curiosity About the People Around Them– people with high EI care about other people and want to know what they are going through. They have the empathy required to relate with others effectively. This also makes it easier for them to understand other people and be a good judge of character. They can read people accurately and see the motivations behind their actions and behavior. To these, they can react accordingly.

Gratefulness– there is always more to be thankful for than to feel wrong about. This is what people with high EI subscribe to. Thinking about what you are grateful for instead of what you do not have is a great mood booster. Studies support this with findings that indicate a 23% reduction in cortisol, a stress hormone, in people who have an attitude of gratitude. As a result, they have more energy and are mentally and physically more capable to do their tasks

Ability to Decide When to Stop and Take A Break– it is not wrong to take a little breather from time to time. People with high EI can muster the self-control to say no to just another hour more of overtime at the office, to taking work during their off days because there are just too many items in the office pipeline, or to taking phone calls in the middle of the night because the graveyard shift personnel do not know what to do.

Emotionally intelligent people know that they need a break from all the stress to function optimally. They can stop and step back from their routine and give their minds and bodies the chance to rest and refocus. This results in an emotional, mental, and physical state ready to get back to things from where they left off.

Belief That No One or Nothing Is Perfect– again, this comes from recognizing that people make mistakes and there are no exceptions. They accept that not all things can be as they expect them to be. They accept the flaws and deal with them in a manner that will give them the best outcomes. They are not too hard on themselves when they make mistakes. Instead, they learn from their mistakes. They adapt and then move on, avoiding the same mistakes along the way.

Ability to Let Go of Excess Baggage– negative thoughts and emotions can be a heavy burden to carry along with you on your road to success. A person with high EI does not hold grudges. He does not allow ill feelings to linger and impair his judgment.

Even toxic people can become excess baggage for you if you do not have the EI to handle them properly. They can weigh you down and infect you with their being "toxic." People with high EI can keep a good head on their shoulders and less steam blowing out of their ears and nose.

Healthy Mind and Body– as negative emotions are kept at bay; highly emotionally intelligent people are less likely to turn to unhealthy coping habits like smoking and drinking. They know that their bodies need proper care if they are to perform at their best every day.

They do not rely on coffee to keep them going as they have enough supply of healthy happy hormones to give them the energy to get through the day. They ensure that their minds and bodies can get the nourishment they need from a balanced diet and lifestyle.

Even when they are "forced" to be around negative people, people with high EI do not let them affect their happiness. They are confident enough with who they are and what they can do and thus do not let other people's opinion cast a cloud over their sunny disposition.

How Emotional Intelligence Is Helpful to Analyze People

Emotional intelligence is beneficial when it comes to dealing with other people. Yes, the general intellect is useful, but you need a substantial level of the EQ to handle social relationships.

EQ is required also in businesses; it helps you understand a better way to close that deal. You'd get to understand your clients better.

It's possible to have a high level of EQ and IQ at the same time. Since IQ deals with your mental capacity and EQ deals with the ability to relate with people, you can very well have it both ways.

Emotional intelligence helps you draw on your reserve. You get to focus on your mental and emotional health and keep an eye on others emotional health.

Chapter 5: Components of Personality

Components

What are the components that make up or define a personality? When we look at the definitions, you'd think that a person's character is made of pieces of patterns and traits. While this is true, it is not entirely what makes a personality. Some other core components of nature are:

- Psychological and physiological: while most approve that personality is a product of psychological form, research also points to nature being influenced by biological needs and processes.
- Consistency: there are a recognizable order and regularity to the behaviors seen. People generally behave or act in the same ways no matter what the situation.
- Multiple expressions: when we speak about personality, it extends above and beyond behaviors. Personality is also perceived in our feelings, thoughts, social interactions as well as our close relationships.
- Behaviors and actions: personality also has a massive effect on what causes us to act, behave, move, and response in specific ways.

Psychology Applications

How personality changes and develops over a person's lifetime is a fascinating element of life that one can study. This study and the results gained serve as an essential tool to understand the real-world practical applications, why people act and behave a certain way, and what motivates the behaviors and thoughts.

In most cases, to study a person's personality, personality assessment tests are usually done to help people understand and learn more about themselves and their weaknesses, preferences, and strengths. These assessments may focus on how people level on certain traits on whether they rank high on conscientiousness, extroversion, and openness. Some reviews, though, focus on specific aspects of personality changes over a course of time, whereas detailed assessments are used to help people determine the kinds of careers that go well with their existing personality and how they can perform specific job tasks.

How Do They Answer Questions?

One important thing to pay attention to when trying to gauge people's personality type is how they answer questions. Extraverts often answer questions quickly and tend to think out loud. This means that they will likely verbalize several thoughts before officially giving their final answer. Alternatively, all of these thoughts may work together to create their overall solution. Introverts on the other hand are far quieter. They may use a filler word such as "um" or "uh" while they think about it, but they are less likely to provide as much information about the thought process. Instead, they will quietly mull it over in their mind until they have an answer for you.

Are They Focused on The Past and Present, Or the Future?

These people are more concerned about right this minute and use the past to create their overall outlook on life. In other words, they combine the past and present to create their perception of reality.

The other type of person is known as an intuitive. Intuitive types are people who are more focused on the future. While they are presently living in the moment, they are likely to be looking for what is coming next, rather than mulling over what has already happened.

How Do They Consider Others in Decisions?

If you want to know what drives a person, pay attention to how they consider other people when making decisions. People who make decisions quickly without considering how the outcome will affect others are known as thinkers. These are people who are more focused on the logical, rational, and thought-based side of things. They are likely not intentionally ignorant toward how the outcome affects others. Instead, they are simply driven by thought. The opposite of this includes those who are driven by their feelings. These people are more likely to pay attention to how the outcome will affect themselves and the other people in their lives. They want to know what the emotional repercussions will be and are very careful to make sure that no one gets hurt due to their actions.

How Do They Adapt to Change?

Some people adapt well to change, others don't. Knowing this element of a person's personality type can significantly help you when it comes to understanding them as a whole. If a person tends to be open to options and is willing to look at all different solutions for a problem, they are more likely to be comfortable with change. They can adapt to any chosen solution and are typically more interested in selecting the best answer for the question than the best solution. The other type, then, is someone who is not good with change. These people choose the solution that answers the question and keeps them feeling comfortable in the solution. They are unlikely to want to change their decision and will typically defend their solution quite gravely.

Combining the answers to these four questions is the best way to gauge how a person is in various situations. You will be able to understand and predict how they are most likely to act under a variety of different circumstances, making it much easier to understand their personality type. Remember, everyone has a different placement on the personality spectrum. Some may be louder and more outgoing than others, whereas others might be quieter and more reserved. They may, however, share qualities from opposite ends of the spectrum. The best way to gauge exact personality type is to look at each person individually and build their baseline with this knowledge.

Chapter 6:   Personality Types

We use the different types of personalities to know the strengths of each person. Let us look at the different kinds of people that you will come across.

Most people have a general idea of being shy, daring, outgoing, or charismatic. But this is not all when you understand the personality type you get to enjoy many benefits:

Knowing Other People's Preferences

Every person has his or her preferences, and you can judge these by knowing the personality type.

When these people operate within the preferences, you get them to be more effective and efficient. However, operating outside the preferences requires more type and energy.

Knowing if you are within the boundaries can improve efficiency, productivity, and even grow management skills.

Avoid Conflict

Understanding the type of person by depending on the personality type helps you avoid any conflict.

You get to diffuse them way before they come up. If you know that your personality makes you intense whenever a situation arises, you will adjust the behavior to be more receptive to the issue.

When you are usually the one to accept responsibility even when you aren't the one that messed things up, you get to train yourself to become more analytical and take time to evaluate the situation before you handle it.

Helps You Appreciate Diversity

Once you know your personality type, you have the chance to interact with other people and appreciate how diverse they are.

When you are in a work environment, the chances are that you will hit a roadblock and end up failing to handle some situations.

When this happens, it is good to have a mind to take up the issue on your behalf and implement it.

Find the Right Career

The personality type you adopt plays a massive role in the kind of job that you are suited to.

It also affects how you handle the job that you are given.

The type of personality you have helps you find the right career to give you proper job satisfaction. For instance, if you are an extrovert, you will find it hard to work in a position that requires you to work alone.

On the other hand, if you are an introvert, you will find it hard to work in a position that doesn't allow you to work alone.

Make Better Decisions

How you make decisions is based more on what you see and experience.

You know that you will either end up with something good or lose out when you take a particular decision.

It also bases on sensing and intuition.

If you decide to make a decision based on sense, you will engage all your fixe senses to gather information, analyze it, and make the right decision.

On the other hand, if you use intuition to decide, you will most likely feel the situation before you can make a choice.

The only downside to analyzing issues before you decide is that you will tend to explore the problems longer than necessary, which in turn decides to take longer than expected.

The theory behind having a personality type is that we get born with it. Then we live with it before finally dying with it.

When faced with a situation, we have the chance to apply the personality type the right way spending on the scenario or experiences

The personality types are based on Myers-Briggs theory developed by a partnership between a mother and daughter combination.

Let us look at the combination pairs that make the theory applicable in all situations:

Extraversion and Introversion

This is concerned with the way you direct your energy.

If your energy is mostly directed towards dealing with people, situations, and things, you are an Extravert (E).

On the other hand, if you direct your energy towards your inner world, you are a perfect example of an introvert (I).

Sensing and Intuition

This looks at the kind of information that you end up processing.

If you are one to look at facts, analyze them, and then come up with a decision from the points, you are a sensor (S).

On the other hand, if you are one that makes your decisions without having to analyze facts, then you are intuitive (N)

Thinking and Feeling

This looks at your personality type, depending on your decision-making style.

If you base your decisions based on logic, taking time to analyze and come up with the best approach, then you prefer Thinking (T).

If on the other hand, you prefer to use values, which means you make decisions based on what you see is essential, then you are in for Feeling (F)

Judgment and Perception

This is the final pair that you can use to determine your personality type.

If you plan your life in a structured way, you prefer Judging (J).

If on the other hand, you have a preference of going along with the flow, responding to things as they come along, then you are in for Perception (P).

To determine the kind of personality you are, you need to take a test that will use the information you give to determine your personality type.

The 16 Personality Types

The Inspector – ISTJ Personality

When you first meet them, ISTJs are usually intimidating.

They look formal, serious, and organized; they uphold tradition and old-school values that make them work hard, be patient, and honour any responsibility that they are given.

They don't make a lot of noise; instead, they are quiet, calm, and reserved.

The Counselor – INFJ Personality

These are ideologists and visionaries that ooze with creative imagination and a lot of brilliant ideas.

They have a good way to look at the world and have a depth to how they think, never accepting things the way they come.

They are usually looked at to be amusing or weird due to their outlook towards life.

The Mastermind – INTJ

These are usually introverts that are reserved and quiet, always comfortable being left alone.

When they socialize, they drain their energy, making them get to recharge.

They don't like coming up with plans and strategies, always being exact at what they do.

The Giver – ENFJ Personality

These are focused so much on other people.

They are usually charismatic, idealistic, ethical, and highly principled.

They know how to connect to other people so well regardless of the background and the personality.

They usually rely on feelings and intuition and mainly rely on imagination rather than the real world.

The Craftsman – ISTP personality

These are usually logical and mysterious but very enthusiastic and spontaneous.

Their personality traits aren't easily recognized, and many people can't anticipate the way they react.

They are usually unpredictable, but they find a way to hide the traits in the world.

The Provider – ESFJ Personality

This is the extrovert.

They are social animals that feed their need to interact with other people and make them happy.

They are usually popular among their circle of friends. These are traditionally sports hero and cheerleaders.

Later in the year, they are the center of planning social events and organizing them for the families.

The Idealist – INFP Personality

These are usually reserved and quiet.

They rarely talk about themselves, especially when they meet with a new person.

They spend most of their time alone and in a quiet place to make sense of the things happening around them.

They don't make decisions before analyzing the situation.

The Performer –ESFP Personality

These are seen to be the entertainers in the group.

They are usually born to be at the front of the group and tend to capture the stage.

They like being in the spotlight and love learning and sharing what they have learned with others.

The Champion – ENFP Personality

These have individualistic characteristics and don't like being forced to live outside what they believe in.

They love being around other people and have a lot of intuition when it comes to themselves and others.

The Doer – ESTP Personality

They have that need for social interaction all the time, and a need for their freedom.

They usually make decisions before they think and are always fixing issues as they move ahead.

The Supervisor – ESTJ Personality

They are honest, organized, and great believers in all that they do.

They always believe that what they indulge in is socially acceptable.

They usually opt to take the post of being the leader of the pack.

The Commander – ENTJ Personality

They focus on the external aspects of things that they deal with rationally and logically.

They are naturally born leaders that take everything to a whole new level.

The Thinker – INTP Personality

They thrive in an environment where the situation needs logic ad brilliant thinking.

They love working according to patterns and have an eye for discrepancies.

The Nurturer – ISFJ Personality

These are usually ready to pay back generosity for generosity, and they believe in making sure that things work the way they need to do.

They value cooperation and harmony when they meet with people.

The Visionary – ENTP Personality

These are rare in the world.

They might not thrive in social situations, especially those involving people that are different from them.

They are knowledgeable and intelligent with the need for mental stimulation most of the time.

The Composer – ISFP Personality

They are introverts but don't behave like one.

They usually have issues connecting with other people at first, but they are fun to be within all situations once they do.

Chapter 7: How to Analyze a Person for Their Photos?

"The camera is an instrument that teaches people how to see without a camera"- Dorothea Lange

There are no escaping people's pictures in the age of a continually buzzing social media feed. Like it or not, people are going to picture of themselves. However, the good news from a person analyzer's perspective is you can gather plenty of clues for speed reading people even before you meet them, only by learning to read their photographs.

Imagine gaining some clues about a prospective employee before they come down for a face or face interview or learning more about a client before negotiating a significant deal with them. How about picking the right date by gathering insights about their personality through their social media images? Every image of a person holds a fascinating amount of information, meaning, and an indication of his or her emotional state. We only have to be conscious enough to watch out for these clues. Sometimes, we are so overcome by the aesthetics of the image or the photography that we miss entirely the image's emotions.

This attempts to offer you some insights about how people's photographs can be used for interpreting their values, personality, and behavioral traits. There are some obvious and some subtle pointers about decoding an individual's personality through their photos. You'll learn to find meaning and context within the images rather than view them as random shots.

Do Not Rush

Since photographs capture moments where time freezes, you need to study the image carefully to avoid any biases or inaccurate readings about something that may have happened in a microsecond. This may be contrary to the fast-speed, short span of attention, limited energy, and the multi-tasking disposition we display. Hit the brain's pause button, do some deep breathing and get yourself into slow motion before you begin analyzing people through their images. You need to approach the art of analyzing people with both curiosity and compassion.

Don't leave out any details. Look at the entire image. What is it that holds your attention when you first look at the picture? What are the conspicuous aspects of the image? Slowly move your attention and awareness to the other parts of the photos. Look at it from different angles and perspectives.

Pull the image closer to your vision to detect elements that would otherwise go unnoticed. There are plenty of subtle details that your eye may miss if you don't view it near. Turning the image upside down or sideways allows you to view it from an unusual perspective, changing your entire viewpoint about the image. You'll end up noticing things you wouldn't have otherwise seen.

Subjective Reactions

What strikes you the most about an image when you see it for the first time? What emotions, feelings, thoughts, and sensations overcome your mind when you look at the picture intuitively? Think of a single descriptive word or phrase as a caption or title for the image that captures your spontaneous reaction.

Do you think the picture represents pride, anger, anxiety, relief, frustration, confinement, exhaustion, success, happiness, exhilaration, smoothness, rage, sadness, and other compelling emotions? Your gut-level reaction offers a clue on what you are thinking about the person.

While observing or analyzing people through their photographs, one of the most important considerations is your instant or immediate reaction. However, you'll need to go beyond the first impression. You'll have to apply some amount of free association to analyze the person. Through free association, you are focusing on all elements of the image. Here are some questions you can ask yourself to facilitate more significant free association to analyze people through images.

What does the picture remind you of?

What is the predominant emotion expressed by the person in the image?

What memories, incidents, and experiences can you pull out from your state of awareness on looking at the image?

How would you title the image?

However, when you are analyzing people through their pictures, beware against what psychologists' terms projection. Projection is an unconscious process through which our feelings, emotions, experiences, and memories distort our perception of other people we are analyzing. You may invariably end up projecting your feelings and experiences to them than trying to identify their personality. This is especially true for more ambiguous images.

You don't know if you are rightly empathizing with people reading them correctly or simply recalling your own experiences.

Sometimes, our subjective reactions get in the way of reading people accurately. However, overcome this tricky situation and identifying when your own experiences and biases are getting in the way of analyzing people will help you be a more effective people analyzer.

Facial Expressions

Human beings are innately expressive when it comes to tuning in to other people's facial expressions. What is your first reaction on looking at the person's face in the photograph? Psychologists have recognized seven basic emotions in a person – surprise, contempt, fear, sadness, anger, disgust and happiness. Keep these seven basic emotions in mind while analyzing people's expressions in images. At times, the expressions are underplayed or subtle, making it challenging to pin down the basic emotion.

Look for pictures where the person may not be aware that they are being clicked since that can be a more accurate representation of their subconscious mind.

Relationships

Again, you can tell a lot about the relationship between people by looking at their photographs. If a person is leaning in another person's direction, there may be attraction or affection between the people. Similarly, if people are leaning in the opposite direction from each other, the relationship may lack warmth. If you notice a person clinging on to their partner's arm in almost every photograph, they may most likely be insecure about losing their partner. It may reveal a deep sense of insecurity or fear of losing their partner.

Try to predict the relationship between people through their body language in images. This can also be done in any public place where you have some time at hand to check people's body language, relationship equation, and reactions. What are their feelings, emotions, thoughts, and attitudes towards each other? Is there a pattern in how people touch, lean towards each other or look at one another? Does their body language reveal a lack of connectedness?

One of my favorite pastimes when it comes to analyzing people is looking at celebrity couples' photographs and trying to read the nature of their relationship and/or their personality through their body language and expressions. I try to analyze if the image reveals intimacy, affection, and positivity? Or it demonstrates tension, disharmony, and conflict? Akeret, a well-known psychologist, believes that a photograph can also predict a relationships' future.

Some signs of comfort include smiling, holding hands, titling head in the direction of their partner. Hip to hip posture may indicate things are going great between the couple. How is the palmer touch? If it is touching with the full hand, the partners are close and affectionate. On the other hand, fingertips or fist touching can be a sign of being distant and reserved. Crossing legs may mean that they weren't very comfortable or open when the picture was taken. If you find a person crossing their arms or legs in almost every photograph, they may be suspicious, doubtful, cynical, and unenthusiastic by nature.

Profile Pictures and Personality Traits

A big body of research suggests that human beings tend to assess one another's personality through a quick glimpse. This is exactly why first impressions are so lasting. It takes us only three to four seconds to form an impression about a person through verbal and non-verbal clues. Sometimes, they may not even say anything and we can subconsciously tune in to personality.

A recent research study reveals that you don't even have to meet a person once to form an opinion about them. All you need is a glance at their Facebook or even Tinder profile picture to gauge their personality. Here are the big five personality traits that are revealed through a person's profile picture.

The big five is pretty much the same to a scientific classification of personalities as Briggs-Myers is for recruitment. This personality approach classifies personalities based on five fundamental traits: introversion-extroversion, agreeableness, openness to new experiences, conscientiousness, and neuroticism.

A glance at your social media profile picture is sufficient for you to rate people correctly on the five fundamental dimensions. In a research conducted by PsyBlog, it was observed through a scientific analysis of the profile pictures of thousands of social media participant personalities that there were very specific and consistent patterns when it came to each of the five personality attributes.

For example, people scoring high on conscientiousness used natural, filter-free, bright, and vibrant images. They were not afraid to express a large number of emotions through their pictures. If fact, they displayed a higher number of emotions through their images than all other personality types.

You'll also find people scoring high on openness taking the most amazing shots. They are creative, innovative, and resourceful. They'll play a lot with applications and filters owing to their creativity. Their pictures will be more artistic, unique, and feature greater contrasts. Generally, people who score high on openness have their face occupy more space than any other feature in the photograph.

Extraversion folks will have perpetually broad smiles plastered on their faces. They will use collages and may surround their profile picture with used vibrant images. On the other hand, simple images with very little color or brightness is a strong indication of neuroticism. According to the blog, these pictures are likely to display a blank expression or in extreme cases may even conceal their face.

Agreeable people may often seem to the nicest people to get along with among all personality types. However, turns out, they aren't great photographers. Agreeable people are known to post unflattering images of themselves! However, even with the poor or unflattering images of themselves, they will be seen smiling or displaying a positive expression. The images will be vibrant, positive, and lively.

Chapter 8:   Read the Facial Micro-Expressions

The micro-expression is an expression that lasts about 2-5 milliseconds derived from an unconscious emotion. By unconscious, we mean that it is understood that the individual only realizes it after expressing it.

The Face May Reveal the Opposite of What a Person Says

The emotions are the same whether you're a housewife, a suicide bomber, or a politician in Japan. The truth may not be what you're talking about. The truth is in the face. A detective arrives from the United States with a revolutionary method in the suitcase. It analyzes facial micro-expressions. And it catches liars.

"Bill Clinton, former president of the United States. He tried to deny the case to the trainee, right? He does not synchronize speech speed with the movement of hands. Usually flashes ten to fifteen times a minute," says Detective Wanderson Castilho.

"Somalia, a Botafogo player, went to the TV to declare that he had been kidnapped. If you notice, the blinks are fast. But then they slow down because the brain does not want to see that lie told," says the detective. "The brain knows the truth."

Cristiano and Carlos, people like you or me, will tell you the most exciting moment they have ever experienced in life.

"The most striking moment of my life was the birth of my son. Because I got into the operating room and she had a cardiac arrest in the middle of that surgery. I see that whole run, I do not understand anything, I just see that. At the same time, it was striking and very tense," says Carlos.

"The most exciting moment was in my wife's delivery, where I went to watch in the operating room. It was a joyful moment, I felt numb, and I took lots of pictures. But even then, something different was happening. My wife was going into cardiac arrest, but I was so anesthetized with my son's remarkable moment that I failed to realize that she was going through a problem. But the situation was circumvented and thank God everything went well," says Cristiano.

"Of course, the two did not live the same story. Only one of them lived through the experience. We asked them to tell the same story so Wanderson could detect which one is lying. Watching the video, do we have any micro-expression that we can detect? At one point, we can see some of Carlos's denials about the story. The face does not fit the case, what happened?" says Wanderson.

The study of human behavior in psychology is a complex task, the techniques to understand other people unfold to cover the most diverse forms of human expression. However, no technique is in itself sufficient to face the complexity of human communication.

Verbal communication accounts for only 7% of human communication. In reality, 93% of human communication occurs nonverbally, through tone of voice, intensity, posture, micro-expressions, gait, etc. Results from more than 40 years of research show evidence that makes interpretations of non-verbal behavior more objective and helps psychologists improve their skills in searching for understanding of the other.

Also, the application of knowledge about facial expressions has been consistently useful for various domains ranging from clinical to business. One objective of this book is to explore the scientific production of facial expressions as a technical possibility for the psychologist's current work, say for example, in Mozambique.

We will seek to discuss research foundations from the work of Paul Ekman, elected one of the 100 most important psychologists of the twentieth century by the American Psychological Association (APA) and considered the greatest scholar of facial behavior.

For elaboration, bibliographic research methodology in the molds designed by the APA was used to research documents and relevant information published in books, videos, newspapers, research reports, dissertations, photos, and interviews from the Paul Ekman Group database library.

Micro-Expressions: Revealing Hidden Frauds and Emotions

Unlike macro-expressions which can last for up to four seconds, micro-expressions are very fast facial expressions that last only a fraction of a second and are recognized in cross-cultural studies. They occur when the person, deliberately or unconsciously, tries to hide their feelings. They were initially described in psychotherapy with depressed patients. Researchers proposed that these expressions occur when people have repressed feelings (hidden from themselves) or deliberately try to hide their feelings (deletion). however, it cannot be determined by the expression alone whether they originated from repression or suppression.

More than 99% of the population cannot identify these signs, including professional groups, psychologists, psychiatrists, neurologists, and police, except secret security agents who show better test performance. However, Ekman and Friesen showed that with training, people can recognize them in real-time. These studies suggest that, by enabling professionals (e.g., psychologists), they are better able to perceive signs they did not perceive before, which directly influences how they conduct or approach the situation.

Physiologically, micro-expressions represent signs of stress, that is, when the cognitive and emotional systems enter into a neural conflict, giving rise to the avoidance of brief physical manifestations. For example, this happens when the person does not believe what he says or feels something different from what he shows. An experiment with university students in the USA showed evidence of evasion of micro-expressions to hide unpleasant emotions linked to experience.

Several behavioral scientists and others have been concerned with fraud detection and the method of understanding this type of behavior. These works interested not only the psychotherapeutic community which is concerned with understanding human emotions but also sectors of the army (like the powers of the I and II GM), criminology, and law.

The traditional form for detecting frauds or lies is based on torture and intimidation, which in turn generates physiological responses of stress, and there is always a risk of error and damage to the subject.

The polygraph is an instrument designed to detect lies, evaluating the tension and pulse of the fingers. Changes in this tension and pulsation rhythm from readings taken at baseline would mean lie signals, which trigger an electric shock to the head as an unpleasant stimulus (punishment). However, the physiological reactions to the test itself are considered problematic, so their validity is questionable.

Humans are considered the best tool for detecting frauds (lies). Studies and statistics show that humans achieve up to 90% accuracy in detecting signs of fraud when trained. The observation of physiological signs, lack of spontaneity in expressions, voice hesitation, skin resistance, and other clues represent measurable signs associated with the contrast between cognition and emotion.

Importance of Expression

Knowledge of recognizing the facial expressions of emotions and micro-expressions is of great importance for understanding intrapersonal management, interpersonal relationships, and the development of emotional intelligence and empathy. A study by Helen Reiss et al. showed that the ability to recognize emotions through brief facial expressions results in better empathy ratings as reported for study group patients than for the control group.

Training in facial expressions also increases awareness of internal emotions, allowing us to recognize when we become emotionally vulnerable, enabling better management of emotions.

Facial Expression and Micro-Expression Application in the Real World

Knowledge about facial expressions has practical multidisciplinary application, the disciplines in which it is important to have the capacity to read the emotional states of others include: psychological assessment for screening of criminals in communities, airports, and terrorism prevention; fraud detection in interviews and or police inquiries, clinical support, and evaluation; marketing and sales; research; television industry, etc.

We will discuss some of these applications in detail as they can be implemented in our context:

A) Police training, inquirers, and criminal issues: Fraud, often carries increased emotional expressions than normal situations (micro-expressions). However, micro-expressions do not say in themselves whether the subject is lying but point to discrepancies between what is said and what is emotionally experienced by the individual. Around the world, security agents and police officers from the USA, Portugal, Brazil, the UK, and several other countries have training on recognizing micro-expressions and body language in their training modules.

Considering the explosion of criminal acts of abduction against civilians in Mozambique, these techniques can be useful as evaluation and behavioral monitoring (e.g. on patrol, inquiries) for law enforcement and public safety agents.

B) Profiling at airports: Several universities which study technology have developed, based on Ekman's studies, tracking systems for facial expressions that allow monitoring of terrorism, drug trafficking, and other suspects. Airports security agents are also trained to obtain these cues through direct observation of body language and facial expressions in particular. This can be taken as a standard of prevention of organized crime and security enhancement, especially considering the precautions that international airports recommend following the September 11 attacks.

C) Health professionals: These professionals can develop a better rapport with patients, interacting in a more humane, empathetic and compassionate way, contributing to the achievement of more accurate diagnoses by obtaining more complete information.

D) Nonverbal language in education: The crucial aspects of student-teacher interaction are non-verbal. Teachers can read their students' facial expressions to get suggestions on lesson progress and plan a more effective process. Likewise, school managers who read their teachers' emotions are more likely to reduce burnout and increase their effectiveness.

E) Development of social skills for special populations: Individuals on the autistic spectrum have benefited greatly from the training that helps them recognize micro-expressions through the ESET (subtle expression training tool). At the opposite end of the spectrum, individuals with schizophrenia tend to have an increased ability to recognize emotions than control groups.

F) Psychological and medical evaluation: Ekman's studies evidenced micro-expressions in interviews of the detachment of depressed patients who attempted suicide. Stuart recalls that most psychopathologies in DSM IV are linked to some kind of emotional alteration (APA, 1994). In the modern conceptualization of emotions it is necessary to consider that changes in nonverbal behavior may be associated with the course, signs, and symptoms of the problem.

Chapter 9:   Verbal vs. Nonverbal Behavior

Language is incredible. As humans, we have an incredibly heightened ability to communicate with one another. This level of communication is a part of why we have been able to advance so far in our evolution. The advancement of our communication results in advancement in our society. We will discuss how our communication is more advanced and the intricacies behind verbal and nonverbal behavior. More importantly, we will define nonverbal and verbal behavior and also give two differences between the two and learn how to analyze the statements that other individuals make verbally. More specifically, we will learn how to analyze these verbal statements using nonverbal language. We will also go into the details of analyzing the nonverbal behavior of those around us.

Defining Nonverbal Behavior

Nonverbal behavior or communication is the subconscious or conscious relaying of ideas or emotions through physical motion or well-known and understood gestures. Messages can be transferred non-verbally through a variety of signals and methods.

The first of these defining signals are methods known as proxemics. Proxemics essentially means the distance between two individuals. The distance between two individuals or proxemics carries a lot of weight in terms of nonverbal communication.

The second method of nonverbal communication is known as kinesics and is simply another word for body language. Kinesics or body language is the transmission of ideas through gestures and often unconscious motions of the body.

Meanwhile, another defining method is known as haptics. Haptics is another word for the act of touching something. In the world of nonverbal behavior, the way that somebody touches something carries a lot of weight in communicating their emotions to another individual. A soft touch on the arm can mean many things, which becomes very different in comparison to a firm grasp of one's hand. Not all touches are equal, and every touch—depending on its longevity, intensity, and location on the body—has many different meanings behind it.

Another form of nonverbal communication is our appearance. People use their appearance to communicate their personality in a variety of ways. Most of this is a conscious decision made by the individual, but some factors are almost entirely caused by our parents that aren't necessarily chosen by us but still say things about ourselves. Most likely, the biggest and most common type of nonverbal communication using our parents is simply judging whether or not somebody cares about their appearance. By just looking at another person, we can instantly tell whether they care about how they appear to them. This carries a huge amount of weight in the snap judgment we make about people every day. The final common form of nonverbal communication is the use of eye contact. Eye contact is extremely important in us as humans. Humans are very focused on an individual's eyes, which is often one of the first things that a person looks at when they see a new face. Your eyes are often considered the windows to the soul, which is true in the sense that they can reveal many factors about yourselves. By looking into someone's eyes or measuring the amount of eye contact they give, we can understand a vast amount of information about their personality. Do they have strong eye contact? Do they avoid eye contact? Do they have intense eye contact? The answers to all of these queries give us different definitions to a person's personality. As humans, we put a lot of weight on an individual's eye contact as a defining portion of their personality. This is why we must keep eye contact in mind when attempting to understand someone's nonverbal communication.

Defining Verbal Communication

Verbal communication seems quite obvious when spoken out loud. Verbal communication consists of any form of speech or language used to relay ideas or thoughts to another. Verbal communication includes much more than simply speaking to a person. The way we string together ideas and thoughts with words shows a lot about their personality in the words that we choose in the cadence that we choose to put them together. There are multiple ways that we can express ourselves through verbal communication. The first and most evident way to express ourselves through verbal communication is by speaking to those around us. By stringing together words and sentences, we create cohesive thoughts and ideas that express our feelings to those around us.

In addition to being able to accurately and positively express our emotions and feelings to those around us, the act of speaking is also quite easy to use to persuade or to alter our true meaning. It is much easier to lie to a person verbally than to lie to a person with our body language. Because of this, we often find people who lie very easily vocally to a person but whose body language cues do not match their words.

The second form of verbal communication, writing, may surprise some people reading this text. While not technically verbal, the act of writing still comprises verbal communication because it uses common vocally spoken language simply in written form. The difficulty in this is that a person reading a text has a much harder time guessing and understanding the cadence of the person who wrote the text. Because of this, written ideas and emotions can be misconstrued because people cannot quite tell the intonation of the author of the text through the words.

Another form of verbal communication is an underlying feeling within our words known as denotation or connotation. The connotation is considered as the feelings or emotions associated with the meanings of certain words or phrases. This is not to be confused with its antonym, denotation, which is the literal or primary meaning of a word, opposite to the emotions or series that the word suggests. To convey these important forms of verbal communication, a person must use our neck form of verbal communication.

The next form of verbal communication that we will be discussing is tone and volume. When talking to another person, an individual's tone can express a lot about that person's inner thoughts or feelings. The tone is a very difficult form of communication to pin down and explain to people. For some individuals, the tone is very easy to control and change in their language—while for others, it can be very difficult. You cannot describe the tone based on the inflection that an individual puts on to certain words at certain times. The tone is very interesting because every person can understand the meaning behind other people's tones almost in perfect connection with one another. Still, it is very difficult to explain to others. In connection to this, a person's volume also holds a great deal of significance in their verbal communication. Since childhood, we have all learned about the difference between an inside voice and an outside voice. Do volume levels show a lot about our emotions? We can read a lot about how someone feels in a certain situation based on their volume at that time.

It is important always to remember that you have to use both verbal and nonverbal forms of communication together in parallel to understand the total outcome of a person's ideas and theories. A common misconception amongst individuals is that verbal communication and nonverbal communication are contradictory. This is not the case. Verbal and nonverbal communication must go side-by-side when communicating with those around us. The combination of these two complex forms of communication makes the translation of our ideas and theories the most effective. One cannot exist without the other—in most cases. Body language specialists often assert that nonverbal communication can play one of five roles when trying to read another person. These five roles are known as substitution, reinforcement, contradiction, accentuation, and regulation.

Substitution - certain types of nonverbal communication are started as a substitution or placement for verbal communication. Examples of this are nodding your head for yes or shrugging your shoulders for "I don't know."

Reinforcement - nonverbal communication can often be used to reinforce a previously given statement. By reading an individual's body language and judging it consistently, you can almost entirely ascertain whether they are telling the truth or not.

Contradiction - this is the opposite of reinforcement. If a person's body language appears to be contradicting something that they are saying, then by the rule of contradiction, they are almost certainly lying—depending on their environment, of course.

Accentuation - body language often serves as a method of accentuating something that a person says vocally. Examples of this include smiling when someone says that they are happy or shivering when somebody says that they are cold. This can also be used to put a greater level of importance to a statement that somebody has given out. An example of this is creating the quotation mark symbol with your fingers while saying something sarcastically. By adding body language to your making statement, you are reaffirming and showing importance in your statement.

Regulation - an individual's body can also serve to regulate that person's vocal language.

Chapter 10: Personal Beliefs

A belief is something that you hold as a fact or truth. Each person has something that they believe in – some good and others bad. A personal belief is a collection of ideas that a person sees as true. In most cases, things that contradict your personal beliefs will often make you angry, frustrated or uncomfortable.

Beliefs come from several sources. These include:

- The environment – your environment is capable of shaping you into believing some things about yourself, others and life in general
- Knowledge – information obtained from people, books and quotes
- Personal experiments and experiences
- Cultural and societal norms such as religious beliefs
- Events – these may help you to establish beliefs. For instance, attending an event may change your perspective about life

In most cases, potential beliefs will stay in your mind until you can embrace them as truths and make them part of your belief system. Before people make these potential beliefs part of them, they take time to find reasons to allow such beliefs on their list. Once an individual accepts a certain belief, they can stand and defend that belief with all the pieces of evidence available.

There is a large difference between beliefs and values. Values represent long-standing beliefs that have proven to be of importance to an individual. Therefore, beliefs are the building blocks of values, which become standards of operation that people use to define their lives and choices. Only beliefs that are important to a person can grow into values. These can then be categorized into various types depending on their role. For instance, you can have values that are related to career, family, wealth or happiness. Being able to differentiate your values is important since you will understand where to apply them in your decision-making processes.

Together with values and beliefs, there is also, what is known as attitude. This is the feeling people have towards each other and the present circumstances. A person's beliefs and attitude contribute greatly to his behavior. People derive their attitude from beliefs and values.

Importance of Personal Beliefs

Beliefs define behavior. Most of the things you do can be easily traced to your beliefs about your surroundings and the world. Beliefs may also influence your reaction to the behavior of others. This is why it is important to ensure that you always choose the right beliefs since they are not private aspects of your life. Below are some roles played by your personal belief:

1. Influences your behavior

Most of your personal beliefs often affect how you perceive and react to some situations. For instance, you may feel offended and react in anger when a person tries to challenge what you have as part of your belief system. Most beliefs affect the human mind and how it responds to certain circumstances.

2. Influences perception

Your beliefs can also impact your perception about everything that goes on around your life. For instance, if you are a person that values the law and observes it, you will always treat those who break the same law as the guilty ones.

3. Influences your choices

Have you ever wondered what influenced your choice of career, spouse, neighborhood, course or diet? There must be an underlying belief somewhere that influenced this decision. It is never a matter of chance or inner wisdom. You only had to think or believe that one choice is better than the other is and that is how you reached your decision. When faced with several things to choose from, people tend to settle for that choice that closely matches their belief. So, your choices greatly reflect some of your beliefs.

4. Influences your personality

People with strong beliefs always display strong personalities. Your belief system determines your personality more than any other factor. For instance, a person who believes that lies are wrong will always endeavor to remain true to others without minding the consequences.

When beliefs are exercised and chosen correctly, they greatly impact a person's character. They also contribute to your growth and development. The more you exercise a certain belief, the more it becomes part of you. Eventually, this belief becomes a component of your nature and you will not need to struggle to implement it. Personal beliefs help individuals to perform better in their personal and corporate worlds. They give you a sense of identity and convict you any time you are about to decide that is contrary to your belief system. When faced with a challenge, your beliefs can act as a motivation that steers you into fighting for your rights. It always becomes peaceful when people know that things are being done based on their belief system.

Beliefs and Human Behavior

Most people tend to go about their daily businesses without understanding what contributes to their behavior. Yet, human behavior's motives are often based on several beliefs that people have created about themselves. These beliefs often determine how people react to situations and how they respond to their emotions and the emotions of others. In a nutshell, your beliefs determine what you do daily and influence how you do it.

Personal beliefs are always very strong. They are responsible even for the career you choose, the relationships you get into and the things you achieve. When asked what beliefs influence their lives, most people are always unable to respond to this question. They would not even know where to begin since they do not have their personal beliefs defined. However, most beliefs are in-born or implicit. This means that other people cannot identify them, yet they do exist and influence a lot of things that go on in the lives of human beings.

Personal beliefs are different from other types of beliefs like religious, secular or political beliefs. These include guidelines that build individual capabilities. Most people seek to gain conscious awareness of these beliefs to influence the outcome of their behaviors. To understand this better, let us look at some of the personal beliefs that influence the totality of a person's wellbeing.

- **Control**

The first and most influential personal belief that human beings have is the degree of control on their future and destiny. Beliefs that revolve around control normally direct you to pursue or stop pursuing some goals for one reason or the other. When control beliefs lose their power in you, you will start linking your accomplishments to luck, fate or circumstance. Individuals who focus on external influencers for their behaviors often avoid setting big goals. They always remain at their comfort level since they are ready to embrace any outcome that results from their behavior.

On the other hand, individuals who have strong control beliefs always command their actions and outcomes. They believe that they can influence the results of anything and focus on their personal growth and development. They understand the role beliefs play in determining their success; therefore, they emphasize the place of self-belief in all their activities and performance. They can tie their successes and failures to certain aspects of their lives and seek to improve their performance each time.

- **Competency Beliefs**

These also influence your behavior in a very big way. They include assessments of your ability to obtain the required outcome. They also indicate the assessment of some abilities and skills necessary to accomplish a certain assignment or purpose.

Competence beliefs may arise from a person's past performance while others may arise from present challenges. People who tend to assess their level of competence do this based on their knowledge and skills and some competency beliefs that include how others perceive an individual. The effectiveness of competency beliefs can be used to determine a person's self-worth. They can be used to determine how a person will perform on a particular role and how he can overcome challenges. Competency assessments are commonly used to determine the capability of a person in a certain skill or ability.

- **Value-Based Beliefs**

Another attribute that influences your personal belief is the amount of value you place on some tasks' outcome. This value differs among individual and cultural standards. It also changes based on the level of social, moral and cognitive development that a person needs.

When you place very little value on a certain task or goal, you will not sacrifice your effort on it. For instance, if a certain career goal is of no value to you, you will not spend time building that career. If you have enrolled in a class associated with the career, you will not see the importance of completing that class and obtaining a certificate over it. Another example is when you are participating in a race and the first position is not of value to you, you will not deliver your best in terms of your pace. You will go at a comfortable pace for you, so long as you reach the finish line.

Assessing values involves understanding how it impacts the person's beliefs and outcomes. There are two types of values that you need to understand.

1.   The intrinsic value which is measured by the level which a person enjoys completing a task

2.   The utility value which refers to the usefulness associated with mastering and completing a task

Personal beliefs that assign very little value on good behavior contribute greatly to some moral disengagements that ruin individuals and organizations' reputations. People with less value on ethics and honesty will always engage in unpleasant personal and business practices without being mindful of the environment and the people around them.

Goal Orientation

Personal belief is also related to how you define and pursue your goals. Goals define a person's capability as well as their purpose for engaging in a certain activity. Setting goals enables you to come up with certain performance targets, which you must meet within a stipulated amount of time. For instance, you may decide to enroll for a course for personal development, for appearance purposes, or just because you want to master a certain skill. These are three different goals.

When you pursue a goal to improve your appearance, your focus is always on being good in your colleagues or friends' eyes. Most people that go for this goal are those that keep comparing themselves with others. They are often driven by the desire to outdo others and do not focus on results.

Epistemological Beliefs

These are personal beliefs that are related to intelligence and natural knowledge. Some research indicates that some individuals believe that they can improve their intelligence by acquiring new knowledge and expanding their viewing things. Understanding this helps explain some individuals' behavior when it comes to negotiation, persuasion, and other skills that are tied to cognitive and emotional intelligence.

CPSIA information can be obtained
at www.ICGtesting.com
Printed in the USA
BVHW041541160221
600148BV00020B/252